The *I Ching* is one of the world's oldest systems of giving advice about the present and looking into the future. Originally from China, it has been used for centuries to reveal all of life's possibilities and directions. Lots of fun when used with guests or sitting alone at home, the easy-to-use *Little Book of I Ching* will help you decide where to go, and with whom. Divided into 64 readings, the *I Ching* will tell you your personal fortune, your true way, your Tao.

Nizan Weisman resides in Israel, the crossroads between East and West. He is the well-known founder of New Age shops, and has translated and written numerous books, allowing his Western readers a glimpse into Eastern cultures.

LITTLE **BIG** BOOK

SERIES:

Basic Numerology
by Lia Robin

Bach Flower Remedies
by David Lord

Dream Interpretation
by Eili Goldberg

I Ching
by Nizan Weisman

The Tarot of Love
by Keren Lewis

Basic Palmistry
by Batia Shorek

**Aura:
Understanding, Seeing and Healing**
by Connie Islin

**The Zodiac:
A Year of Signs**
by Amanda Starr

LITTLE **BIG** BOOK
of

I Ching

by   Nizan   Weisman

Astrolog Publishing House

Astrolog Publishing House
P.O. Box 1123, Hod Hasharon 45111, Israel
Tel./Fax: 972-9-7412044
E-Mail: info@astrolog.co.il
Astrolog Web Site: www.astrolog.co.il

ISBN 965-494-049-3

Published by Astrolog Publishing House 1998

Distribution:
U.S.A. & CANADA by APG -
Associated Publishers Group
U.K. & EUROPE by DEEP BOOKS
EAST ASIA by CKK Ltd.

Printed in Israel
10 9 8 7 6 5 4 3 2 1

The *I Ching (The Book of Changes)* is a method developed by the Chinese philosopher Fu Hsi to predict the future.

The method is based on the *Tao*. The *Tao* is divided into *Yin* and *Yang*, each of which is divided into two "seasons", and each season into two elements. Since each division is characterized by a short line, either unbroken or broken, we arrive at eight trigrams. Two trigrams are superimposed to create a hexagram. There are 64 possible combinations of hexagrams, constituting all the possibilities in the *I Ching*.

Each hexagram is characterized by a name, serial number, judgment and image. These elements teach the user how to reach the correct answer to his questions or inquiries regarding the future by means of concentration and thought.

In order to find the appropriate hexagram, you should take a coin, decide which side represents "unbroken" and which represents "broken," throw the coin six times and draw the resulting hexagram from bottom to top. Next, identify the hexagram according to the *Key for Identifying Hexagrams* at the end of the book, read the name, judgment and image and mull them over until you obtain the correct answer.

For example: My question is, should I change my job?

I think about the question, take a coin and flip it. It falls on the "broken" side. I draw a broken line. ▬ ▬ The second throw produces another broken line. Above the previous line, I draw a second broken line and receive ▬▬ ▬▬ The third throw gives me an unbroken line, which I draw. The trigram will be ▬▬▬ This is the lower trigram. In the table on page 71, it appears as the fourth from the top in the vertical column. Now I flip the coin three more times and draw another trigram from bottom to top. Let's say that I received ▬▬▬ That is, unbroken, broken, unbroken; this is the upper trigram, and it is the seventh from the left in the horizontal column on page 71. The meeting point of the two trigrams creates the hexagram, and it will be number 56. I open the book on hexagram number 56 (page 62) and read. This hexagram deals with the encounter between fire (constant change) and mountain (stability). This is exactly the problem which I am facing: Should I change my job, or remain in a fixed, stable place? Perusing the chapters of the I Ching will direct me - in this case, toward changing jobs.

Two additional examples can be seen on page 72.

1
Ch'ien

The Creative

Upper trigram: *Ch'ien* – The creative, heaven.
Lower trigram: *Ch'ien* – The creative, heaven.

Judgment:
The works of the creative. Glorious success.
Perseverance will be rewarded.

Image:
Powerful are the forces of heaven at work.
So too the great man devotes himself to endless
activity.

2
K'un

The Receptive
Upper trigram: *K'un* – The receptive, earth.
Lower trigram: *K'un* – The receptive, earth.

Judgment:
The receptive brings with him glorious success.
Mare-like perseverance will be rewarded.
If a man of merit undertakes something and
chooses his own path, he will go astray.
But if he is willing to follow, he will find guidance.
It is advisable to find friends in the south and the
west and to forego friends in the east and the
north.
Calm perseverance will lead to good fortune.

Image:
The characteristic of the earth is receptive
devotion. So it is with the great man, too. His great
excellence carries the world.

3
Chun

Difficulties at the Beginning
Upper trigram: *K'an* – The abysmal, water.
Lower trigram: *Chên* – The arousing,
shock, thunder.

Judgment:
The action of difficulties at the beginning.
Glorious success.
Perseverance will be rewarded.
Do not pursue any objective.
It would be good to appoint helpers.

Image:
Clouds and storms: These are the image of
difficulties at the beginning. So too the great
man brings order into confusion.

4
Mêng

Youthful Folly

Upper trigram: *Kên* – Keeping still, mountain.
Lower trigram: *K'an* – The abysmal, water.

Judgment:
Youthful folly is good luck.
It is not I who seek the inexperienced youth.
The youth sought and found me.
I will read the signs to him and explain what
they mean.
If he asks twice or three times, I will know that
he is tiresome and demanding, and I do not
teach those who are tiresome and demanding.
Perseverance will be rewarded.

Image:
A spring welling up at the foot of the mountain:
This is the image of youthful folly. So it is with
the great man, too. He strives to behave in a
decisive manner and cultivates his excellence.

5
Hsü

Waiting (Nourishment)
Upper trigram: *K'an* – The abysmal, water.
Lower trigram: *Ch'ien* – The creative, heaven.

Judgment:
Waiting accompanied by honesty will lead to glorious success.
Perseverance and stability will lead to good fortune.
It would be good to cross the great river.

Image:
Clouds rising up to the heavens: This is the image of waiting.
So it is with the great man, too.
He spends his time eating and drinking and enjoying the pleasures of life.

6
Sung

Conflict

Upper trigram: *Ch'ien* – The creative, heaven.
Lower trigram: *K'an* – The abysmal, water.

Judgment:
Conflict. If you are sincere in your struggle and encounter opposition and obstacles, walking cautiously will bring good fortune.
If you go on to the end, it will bring misfortune.
It would be good to see the face of a great man, but the great river must not be crossed.

Image:
Heaven and water opposed to each other: This is the image of conflict.
So too the great man considers his steps prior to taking action. The situation is extremely dangerous and must be dealt with. The assistance that is on the way is unexpected. However, the dangerous situation does not allow one to be selective.

7
Shih

The Army

Upper trigram: *K'un* – The receptive, earth.
Lower trigram: *K'an* – The abysmal, water.

Judgment:
The army. With perseverance and a strong,
experienced man, good fortune will prevail,
without fail.

Image:
Frozen water on land: This is the image of the
army.
So too the great man educates the masses,
nourishes them and takes care of them with
tenderness and compassion.

8
Pi

Holding Together (Union)
Upper trigram: *K'an* – The abysmal, water.
Lower trigram: *K'un* – The receptive, earth.

Judgment:
Holding together is good fortune!
It would be good to consult with our oracle
about our consistency, our ability to persevere
and our excellence – for then there will be no
mistake.
Those who hesitate and worry gather together,
those who dawdle will meet with misfortune.

Image:
Water gathering on the earth: This is the image
of holding together. So too were the rulers in
former times. They founded the different states
and cultivated friendly relations with the feudal
lords.

9
Hsiao
Ch'u

The Taming Power of the Small
Upper trigram: *Sun* – The gentle, wind.
Lower trigram: *Ch'ien* – The creative, heaven.

Judgment:
The taming power of the small – success!
Dense clouds, but no rain falls on the western
frontier.

Image:
A wind blowing across the heavens: This is the
image of the taming power of the small. So too
the great man cultivates the external aspects of
his excellence.

**10
Lu**

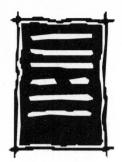

Treading (conduct)
Upper trigram: *Ch'ien* – The creative, heaven.
Lower trigram: *Tui* – The joyous, lake.

Judgment:
Treading.
Treading on the tail of the tiger and it does not
bite – success!

Image:
Heaven above, the lake below: This is the image
of treading from without.
So it is with the great man, too. Situated between
high and low, fulfilling the will of the people.

11
T'ai

Peace

Upper trigram: *K'un* – The receptive, earth.
Lower trigram: *Ch'ien* – The creative, heaven.

Judgment:
Peace.
The small disappears, the great approaches.
Good fortune and success.

Image:
The union of heaven and earth: This is the
image of peace.
So the ruler, in accordance with nature, conducts
himself.
Bestowing their gifts, he improves the lot of the
people.

12
P'i

Standstill (stagnation)
Upper trigram: *Ch'ien* – The creative, heaven.
Lower trigram: *K'un* – The receptive, earth.

Judgment:
Standstill. The lack of understanding amongst
people makes it difficult for a man of merit to
persist on his straight path. The great departs
and the small approaches.

Image:
Heaven and earth are unable to unite: This is the
image of standstill. So too the great man
withdraws into his inner self and exercises
restraint in the expression of his external
excellence. In this way, he protects himself from
the difficulties around him and resists the
temptations of wealth and honor.

13
T'ung
Jên

Fellowship with men
Upper trigram: *Ch'ien* – The creative, heaven.
Lower trigram: *Li* – The clinging, fire.

Judgment:
Fellowship for all to see – success!
It would be good to cross the great river.
A man of merit's perseverance will be rewarded.

Image:
Heaven uniting with fire: This is the image of
fellowship with men.
So it is with the great man, too. He organizes the
clans and relates to everything according to its
nature.

14
Ta
Yü

Possession in Great Measure
Upper trigram: *Li* – The clinging, fire.
Lower trigram: *Ch'ien* – The creative, heaven.

Judgment:
Many possessions – supreme success!

Image:
Fire in heaven: This is the image of many
possessions. So too the great man eradicates evil,
promotes and reinforces good. In so doing, he
obeys the benevolent will of heaven.

15 Ch'ien

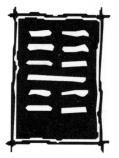

Modesty
Upper trigram: *K'un* – The receptive, earth.
Lower trigram: *Kên* – Keeping still, mountain.

Judgment:
Modesty – success!
A man of merit takes things to their desired
conclusion.

Image:
A mountain as the center of the earth: This is the
image of modesty.
So too the great man decreases that which is too
much, and increases that which is too little. He
examines everything according to its nature and
thereby brings equality.

16
Yü

Enthusiasm

Upper trigram: *Chên* – The arousing, shock, thunder.

Lower trigram: *K'un* – The receptive, earth.

Judgment:

Enthusiasm, it is advisable to appoint helpers and let the troops advance.

Image:

A storm thundering upon the earth: This is the image of enthusiasm. So it was with the rulers in former times, too. They composed music and honored excellence in order to express their appreciation to the Supreme Deity, inviting their ancestors to be present.

17
Sui

Following
Upper trigram: *Tui* – The joyous, lake.
Lower trigram: *Chên* – The arousing, shock, thunder.

Judgment:
Following glorious success.
Perseverance will be rewarded – without fail.

Image:
A storm raging in the middle of the lake: This is the image of following. So it is with the great man, too. He withdraws into his house after nightfall and rests in serenity.

18
Ku

Work on what has been spoiled (decay)
Upper trigram: *Kên* – Keeping still, mountain.
Lower trigram: *Sun* – The gentle, wind.

Judgment:
Work on what has been spoiled – glorious success.
It would be good to cross the great river.
Three days before the starting point.
Three days after the starting point.

Image:
The wind blowing at the foot of the mountain:
This is the image of work on what has been spoiled. So it is with a great man, too. He arouses the people and strengthens their spirit.

31
Hsien

Influence (wooing)
Upper trigram: *Tui* – The joyous, lake.
Lower trigram: *Kên* – Keeping still, mountain.

Judgment:
Influence. Success.
Perseverance will be rewarded. Taking a maiden
as a wife brings good fortune.

Image:
A lake on the mountain: This is the image of
influence. So too the great man encourages
people to approach him by being open to them.

32
Hêng

Duration
Upper trigram: *Chên* – The arousing, shock,
thunder.
Lower trigram: *Sun* – The gentle, wind.

Judgment:
Duration. Success without fault.
Perseverance will be rewarded.
Movement in any direction will be beneficial.

Image:
A storm accompanied by wind: This is the image
of duration. So too the great man stands firm
and does not change his direction.

33
Tun

Retreat
Upper trigram: *Ch'ien* – The creative, heaven.
Lower trigram: *Kên* – Keeping still, mountain.

Judgment:
Retreat. Success.
Perseverance in minor matters will be rewarded.

Image:
Mountain under heaven: This is the image of
retreat. So too the great man keeps his distance
from inferior men. This is not done in anger, but
with forbearance.

34
Ta
Chuang

The Power of the Great
Upper trigram: *Chên* – The arousing, shock,
thunder.
Lower trigram: *Ch'ien* – The creative, heaven.

Judgment:
The power of the great.
Perseverance will be rewarded.

Image:
A storm in the heavens: This is the image of the
power of the great. So too the great man never
treads a path which lacks respectability.

35
Chin

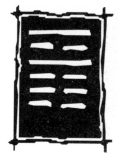

Progress
Upper trigram: *Li* – The clinging, fire.
Lower trigram: *K'un* – The receptive, earth.

Judgment:
Progress. A powerful prince is presented with many horses.
During the course of one day he is granted three audiences.

Image:
Fire rising above the earth: This is the image of progress. So too the great man shines and polishes his glorious virtue.

36
Ming
I

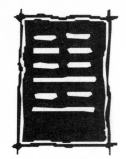

Darkening of the Light
Upper trigram: *K'un* – The receptive, earth.
Lower trigram: *Li* – The clinging, fire.

Judgment:
Darkening of the light. Perseverance when
encountering difficulties will be rewarded.

Image:
Light hidden in the earth: This is the image of
darkening of the light. So too the great man
leads the people. He conceals his light, yet it still
shines through.

37
Chia
Jên

The Family (The Clan)
Upper trigram: *Sun* – The gentle, wind.
Lower trigram: *Li* – The clinging, fire.

Judgment:
The family.
The perseverance of the woman will be
rewarded.

Image:
Wind rising from fire: This is the image of the
family. So it is with the great man, too. His
words are rich in significance and his behavior is
consistent.

38
K'uei

Opposition. Alienation
Upper trigram: *Li* – The clinging, fire.
Lower trigram: *Tui* – The joyous, lake.

Judgment:
Opposition.
Good fortune in minor matters.

Image:
Fire above and the lake below: This is the image
of opposition. So it is with the great man, too.
Even when he is with others, he maintains his
independence.

39
Chien

Obstruction

Upper trigram: *K'an* – The abysmal, water.
Lower trigram: *Kên* – Keeping still, mountain.

Judgment:
South-west shines upon you, but north-east does not.
It would be good to see the face of a great man.
Perseverance will lead to good fortune.

Image:
Water on the mountain: This is the image of obstruction. So it is with the great man, too. He turns his attention to himself and cultivates his excellence.

40
Hsieh

Deliverance

Upper trigram: *Chên* – The arousing, shock, thunder.

Lower trigram: *K'an* – The abysmal, water.

Judgment:

Deliverance. South-west shines upon you. If there is no reason to go forward, going back will lead to good fortune.

If there is a reason to go forward, making haste will lead to good fortune.

Image:

Storm and rain: This is the image of deliverance. So too the great man forgives mistakes and is merciful towards criminals.

41
Sun

Decrease
Upper trigram: *Kên* – Keeping still, mountain.
Lower trigram: *Tui* – The joyous, lake.

Judgment:
Decreasing combined with sincerity – supreme,
unchanging good fortune.
One may continue persevering.
It would be good to strive to achieve some
objective.
How is this to be accomplished?
Two small offering bowls will do.

Image:
A lake at the foot of the mountain: This is the
image of decreasing. So it is with the great man,
too. He controls his anger and curbs his
impulses.

**42
I**

Increase
Upper trigram: *Sun* – The gentle, wind.
Lower trigram: *Chên* – The arousing,shock,
thunder.

Judgment:
Increase. It would be good to strive to achieve
some objective.
It would be good to cross the great river.

Image:
A stormy wind: This is the image of increasing.
So it is with the great man, too. If he sees good,
he imitates it. If he sees evil, he corrects it.

43
Kuai

Breakthrough (Resoluteness)
Upper trigram: *Tui* – The joyous, lake.
Lower trigram: *Ch'ien* – The creative, heaven.

Judgment:
A breakthrough. Be decisive in making the
matter known when an announcement is made in
the royal court.
It must be told truthfully, being aware of the
dangers.
One must warn one's own town, but it would not
be good to resort to arms.
It would be good to strive to achieve some
objective.

Image:
A lake carried to heaven: This is the image of a
breakthrough. So it is with the great man, too.
He distributes his riches to those beneath him
and is never complacent about his excellence.

44
Kuo

Coming to Meet

Upper trigram: *Ch'ien* – The creative, heaven.
Lower trigram: *Sun* – The gentle, wind.

Judgment:
Coming to meet. The maiden is powerful and
very strong.
Do not marry her.

Image:
Wind under heaven: This is the image of coming
to meet. So too does the ruler act, disseminating
his commands and proclaiming them to the four
corners of the world.

45
Ts'ui

Gathering Together (Massing)
Upper trigram: *Tui* – The joyous, lake.
Lower trigram: *K'un* – The receptive, earth.

Judgment:
Gathering together, success.
The king approaches his temple.
It would be good to see the face of a great man;
this would lead to success.
Perseverance will be rewarded.
Great sacrifices will lead to success.
It would be good to strive to achieve some
objective.

Image:
A lake on the earth: This is the image of
gathering together. So it is with the great man,
too. He mends his weapons and braces himself
for the unknown.

46
Shêng

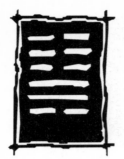

Pushing Upward
Upper trigram: *K'un* – The receptive, earth.
Lower trigram: *Sun* – The gentle, wind.

Judgment:
Pushing upward. Glorious success.
It is essential to see the face of a great man in
order to prevent worry.
Moving southwards will bring good fortune.

Image:
A grove growing in the center of the earth: This
is the image of pushing upward. So too is the
great man who has a devoted nature. He collects
small things in order to obtain something great.

47
K'un

Oppression (Exhaustion)
Upper trigram: *Tui* – The joyous, lake.
Lower trigram: *K'an* – The abysmal, water.

Judgment:
Oppression. Success.
Perseverance will bring good fortune to the one
who is truly great, without fail.
Even when something is said, it will not be
believed.

Image:
A lake with no water: This is the image of
exhaustion. So too the great man risks his life
striving to fulfill his desire.

48
Ching

The Well
Upper trigram: *K'an* – The abysmal, water.
Lower trigram: *Sun* – The gentle, wind.

Judgment:
The well. The town may be changed, but not the
well. It does not decrease or increase.
People come and go and draw water from the
well. If one almost reaches the water but the rope
is too short or the jug breaks, it means
misfortune.

Image:
Water over wood: This is the image of the well.
So it is with the great man, too. He spurs the
people on at their work and encourages them to
help one another.

49
Ko

Revolution
Upper trigram: *Tui* – The joyous, lake.
Lower trigram: *Li* – The clinging, fire.

Judgment:
Revolution. Only at its end will it be believed.
Glorious success.
Perseverance will be rewarded.
Remorse disappears.

Image:
Fire in the lake: This is the image of revolution.
So it is with the great man, too. He determines
the calendar and clarifies the coming of the
seasons.

50
Ting

The Cauldron
Upper trigram: *Li* – The clinging, fire.
Lower trigram: *Sun* – The gentle, wind.

Judgment:
The cauldron.
Great progress and success.

Image:
Fire consuming a branch: This is the image of
the cauldron. So it is with the great man, too. He
fortifies his position by his appropriate
demeanor.

51
Chên

The Arousing, Shock, Thunder

Upper trigram: *Chên* – The arousing, shock,
thunder.

Lower trigram: *Chên* – The arousing, shock,
thunder.

Judgment:
The arousing. Success.
The storm approaches with a terrible noise,
laughing, shouting and spreading fear for a
hundred miles around.
But he does not let the ceremonial wine spill.

Image:
A long-lasting storm: This is the image of shock.
So it is with the great man, too. While he is
trembling and fearful, he reforms his way of life
and examines his mistakes.

52
Kên

Keeping Still, Mountain

Upper trigram: *Kên* – Keeping still, mountain.
Lower trigram: *Kên* – Keeping still, mountain.

Judgment:
Keeping still. Sitting with his back still so that he
no longer feels his body.
When entering the courtyard, he does not see his
people.
Without fault.

Image:
Mountain beside mountain: This is the image of
keeping still. So it is with the great man, too. He
does not permit his thoughts to go beyond his
present situation.

53
Chien

Development (Gradual Progress)
Upper trigram: *Sun* – The gentle, wind.
Lower trigram: *Kên* – Keeping still, mountain.

Judgment:
Development.
The maiden is married.
Good fortune.
Perseverance will be rewarded.

Image:
A tree on the mountain: This is the image of
development. So it is with the great man, too. He
abides in dignity and excellence, guiding the
people towards the good.

54
Kuei
Mei

The Marrying Maiden

Upper trigram: *Chên* – The arousing,shock, thunder.

Lower trigram: *Tui* – The joyous, lake.

Judgment:

The marrying maiden. Progress will lead to misfortune.

Nothing will shine upon you.

Image:

A storm on the lake: This is the image of the marrying maiden. So it is with the great man, too. He is aware of his mistakes in view of his ultimate objective.

55
Fêng

Abundance (Fullness)
Upper trigram: *Chên* – The arousing (shock, thunder).
Lower trigram: *Li* – The clinging, fire.

Judgment:
Abundance. Success.
The king reaches the point of abundance.
Do not be sad.
Be like the sun at midday.

Image:
Simultaneous thunder and lightening: This is the image of abundance. So it is with the great man, too. He rules in legal matters and metes out the appropriate punishment.

56
Lü

The Wanderer
Upper trigram: *Li* – The clinging, fire.
Lower trigram: *Kên* – Keeping still, mountain.

Judgment:
The wanderer. Success in minor matters.
Perseverance will bring good fortune to the
wanderer.

Image:
Fire on the mountain: This is the image of the
wanderer. So it is with the great man, too. He is
cautious and clear-headed when meting out
punishments, and does not allow legal cases to
drag on.

**57
Sun**

The Gentle, Wind
Upper trigram: *Sun* – The gentle, wind.
Lower trigram: *Sun* – The gentle, wind.

Judgment:
Gentleness. Success in minor matters.
Movement in any direction will be beneficial.
It would be good to see the face of a great man.

Image:
Wind follows wind: This is the image of the
gentle wind. So it is with the great man, too. He
disseminates his commands time and time again,
and accomplishes his tasks.

58
Tui

The Joyous (Lake)
Upper trigram: *Tui* – The joyous, lake.
Lower trigram: *Tui* – The joyous, lake.

Judgment:
The joyous. Success.
Perseverance will be rewarded.

Image:
One lake upon another: This is the image of the
joyous. So it is with the great man, too. He joins
his friends for discussion and practice.

59
Huan

Dispersion (Dissolution)
Upper trigram: *Sun* – The gentle, wind.
Lower trigram: *K'an* – The abysmal, water.

Judgment:
Dispersion. Success.
The king reaches his temple.
It would be good to cross the great river.
Perseverance will be rewarded.

Image:
Wind blowing on the water: This is the image of
dispersion. This is what the rulers in former
times would do when they sacrificed to the Lord
and built temples.

60
Chieh

Limitation
Upper trigram: *K'an* – The abysmal, water.
Lower trigram: *Tui* – The joyous, lake.

Judgment:
Limitation. Success.
Severe, rigid limitation must not continue for a
long time.

Image:
Water on the surface of the lake: This is the
image of limitation. So it is with the great man,
too. He determines numbers and measures, and
examines the nature of excellence and correct
conduct.

61
Chung
Fu

Inner Truth
Upper trigram: *Sun* – The gentle, wind.
Lower trigram: *Tui* – The joyous, lake.

Judgment:
The inner truth. Fish and pigs.
Good fortune.
It would be good to cross the great water.
Perseverance will bring reward.

Image:
Wind on the lake: This is the image of the inner
truth. So it is with the great man, too. When he
sits in judgment, he carefully considers the case
and stays executions.

62
Hsiao
Kuo

Preponderance of the Small
Upper trigram: *Chên* – The arousing, shock, thunder.
Lower trigram: *Kên* – Keeping still, mountain.

Judgment:
Preponderance of the small. Success. Perseveranc
will be rewarded. Small objectives may be
achieved, but not great things.
The flying bird brings the message.
It is better to remain down below than strive to
reach the heavens.
Glorious good fortune.

Image:
A storm on the mountain: This is the image of the
preponderance of the small. So it is with the great
man, too. In his conduct he preponderates
humility. In his bereavement he preponderates
grief, and in his personal expenditures, he
preponderates thrift.

63
Chi
Chi

After Completion
Upper trigram: *K'an* – The abysmal, water.
Lower trigram: *Li* – The clinging, fire.

Judgment:
After completion. Success in minor matters.
Perseverance will be rewarded.
Good fortune at first, disorder at the end.

Image:
Water over fire: This is the image after
completion. So it is with the great man, too. He
thinks about misfortune and takes precautions
against it.

64 Wei Chi

Before Completion
Upper trigram: *Li* – The clinging, fire.
Lower trigram: *K'an* – The abysmal, water.

Judgment:
Before completion. Success.
But if the little fox gets his tail wet before
completing the crossing, nothing will shine down
upon you.

Image:
Fire on the water: This is the image before
completion. So it is with the great man, too. He
is careful to differentiate between things so that
each finds its own place.

Key for Identifying the Hexagrams

Upper Trigram → Lower Trigram ↓	Ch'ien ☰	Chên ☳	K'an ☵	Kên ☶	K'un ☷	Sun ☴	Li ☲	Tui ☱
Ch'ien ☰	1	34	5	26	11	9	14	43
Chên ☳	25	51	3	27	24	42	21	17
K'an ☵	6	40	29	4	7	59	64	47
Kên ☶	33	62	39	52	15	53	56	31
K'un ☷	12	16	8	23	2	20	35	45
Sun ☴	44	32	48	18	46	57	50	28
Li ☲	13	55	63	22	36	37	30	49
Tui ☱	10	54	60	41	19	61	38	58

Example: Should I get married?

I flip the coin. The first three throws produce the following lines: unbroken, unbroken, broken, and therefore the first trigram is (from bottom to top) ☱ This is the last trigram in the vertical column on page 71. I flip the coin three more times and get broken, broken, unbroken ☶. This is the fourth trigram on the left in the horizontal row on page 71. The meeting point between the two trigrams produces hexagram number 41. This hexagram (on page 47 in the book) indicates that in stability (family), there is happiness and enjoyment. Note the sentence, "Two small offerings", and think about the meaning of the word "two" in this sentence.

Example: Let's say that the question is: Should I loan money to my friend?

The first three throws produce unbroken, unbroken, unbroken. ☰ This is the lower trigram. The next three throws produce unbroken, broken, unbroken. ☲ This is the upper trigram. Together they create hexagram number 14 (page 20). Reading about it ("Many possessions" ...), we remember that friendship has as much value as money has.